AMAZING ANIMALS

# ALPACAS

BY MARI BOLTE

CREATIVE EDUCATION • CREATIVE PAPERBACKS

Published by Creative Education
and Creative Paperbacks
P.O. Box 227, Mankato, Minnesota 56002
Creative Education and Creative Paperbacks
are imprints of The Creative Company
www.thecreativecompany.us

Design by The Design Lab
Production by Blue Design
Art direction by Graham Morgan

Images by Getty Images/Artur Debat, 23, Hal Beral, 6, IzaLysonArts / 500px, 10, Jan Miracky/robertharding, 13, Matthias Clamer, 21; Pexels/Dmitry Zvolskiy, 20, Matej Bizjak, 17, Trace Hudson, 5; Unsplash/Alec Favale, 16, Arne Verbist, 2, Josiah Farrow, cover, 1, Manuel Keller, 18, Sébastien Goldberg, 9, Yucel Moran, 14; Wikimedia Commons/Cgoodwin, 7, Johann Dréo, 8



Cataloging-in-Publication data is available from the Library of Congress.
Library Binding ISBN: 9798895810507
Paperback ISBN: 9798896800033
eBook ISBN: 9798895811764
LCCN: 2025011184

Printed in China

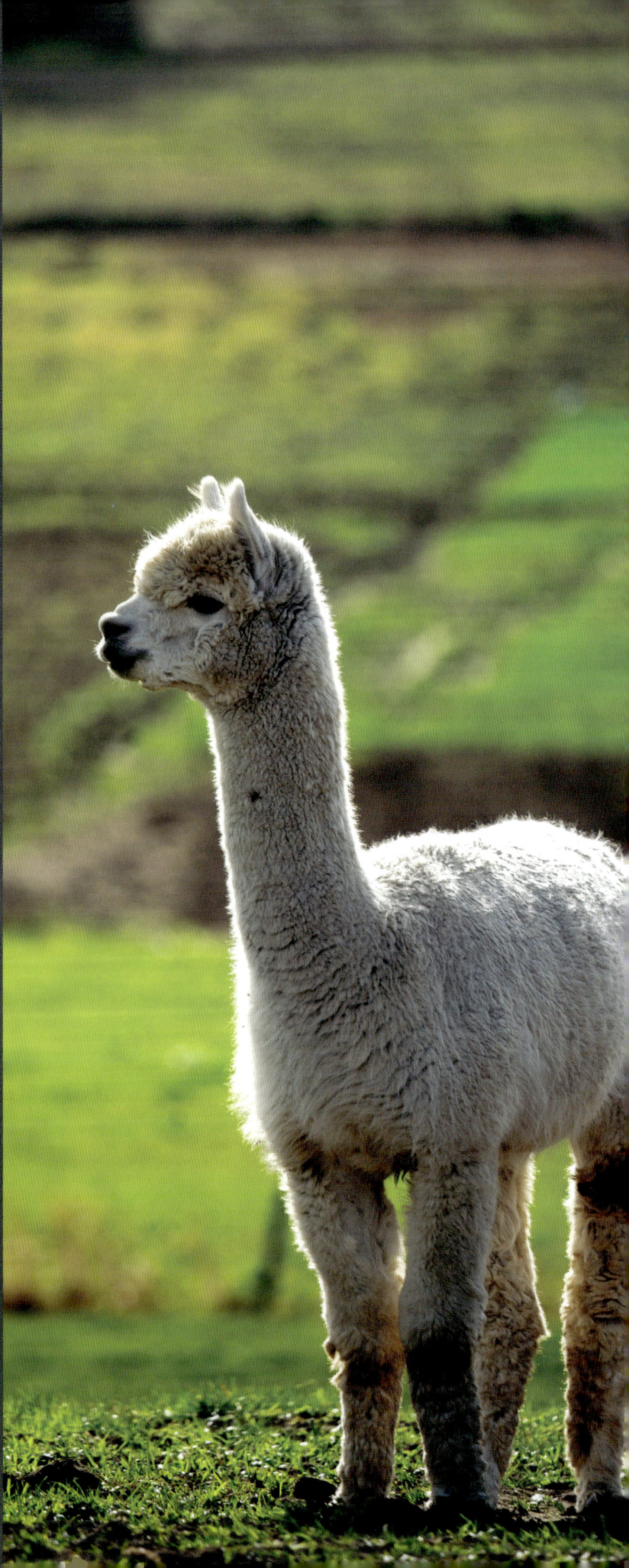

# Table of Contents

**Alpacas** are furry, four-legged animals with long legs, thin necks, and cute faces. They are members of the camelid family. Llamas and camels are in the same family. Alpacas come from the Andes Mountains in South America. Today, they are found around the world.

*Alpacas are raised by people. That means there are no alpacas in the wild.*

*Alpaca hair is called fleece or fiber, not wool or fur.*

There are two kinds of alpacas. The more common kind is the huacaya. It has fluffy, wooly fleece. The other kind is the suri. It has longer fleece that looks like **dreadlocks**. Alpacas come in 22 colors, including white, silver gray, rose gray, and fawn.

**dreadlocks** ropelike hair that is matted, braided, or twisted

Adult alpacas can weigh from 100 to 200 pounds (45.4–90.7 kilograms). They stand between 32 and 40 inches (81.3–101.6 centimeters) tall at the shoulder. Alpacas also have long tails. They can be up to 10 inches (25.4 cm) long.

*From head to toe, alpacas stand around 5 feet (1.5 meters) tall.*

Alpacas can live almost anywhere. They prefer cooler weather, but can do well in hot, damp environments, too. There are between three and four million alpacas around the world. Most of them live in Peru and Bolivia.

*Fleece keeps alpacas warm in cold weather and cool in hot weather.*

*Pet alpacas love treats! They eat all kinds of fruits and vegetables, including apples, bananas, pumpkins, and carrots.*

Alpacas **graze** on grasses or hay. They also munch on brush, trees, or other mountain plants. Their feet have two toes with a pointy nail at the end. The nail grips the ground. They walk on soft foot pads. This lets them graze without damaging the grass.

**graze** to eat throughout the day

Alpacas usually live between 15 and 20 years. Female alpacas can be bred as early as 14 months. Males need a little more time. Some are not fully grown until around two to three years. Alpacas can mate any time of the year.

*If a female is already pregnant, she will spit at males to tell them to stay away.*

After around 350 days, alpacas give birth. Babies are called crias. They weigh between 15 and 20 pounds (6.8–9 kg). Usually, only one cria is born at a time. It can stand and walk less than an hour after birth. It drinks its mother's milk for six months.

*Some alpacas are pregnant for around 320 days. But others go past 380!*

Some farmers use alpacas as guard animals. They are not big enough to scare off large predators. But they will let out a high-pitched scream when they sense danger. They will also bite or kick any predator that gets too close.

*Alpacas are farm animals. Their fleece, meat, and even their poop can be bought and sold.*

Alpacas express their feelings in several ways. Head, neck, and ear positioning is one. Tail swishing is another. Alpacas hum to their babies. They also hum to talk to the rest of the herd. Watch out! Upset alpacas may spit!

*Alpaca spit is part saliva, part undigested food. It is green and doesn't taste good.*

*An Alpaca Tale*

# The people

of Peru believe in giving and taking from nature equally. Legend says that a god brought alpacas as a gift to the people. They would keep people warm with their fleece. In exchange, people would take good care of alpacas forever. But if people did not take care of alpacas, the god would take them away.

# Read More


Dittmer, Lori. *Machu Picchu*. Mankato, MN: Creative Education and Creative Paperbacks, 2025.

Jameson, Karen. *A Llama is Not an Alpaca: And Other Mistaken Animal Identities*. New York: Running Press Kids, 2023.

Tillotson, Carrie. *Alpacas Here, Alpacas There*. New York: Beach Lane Books, 2025.


# Websites

Britannica Kids: Alpaca
*https://kids.britannica.com/kids/article/alpaca/352739*
Learn more about these cuddly creatures.

Smithsonian's National Zoo: Alpaca
*https://nationalzoo.si.edu/animals/alpaca*
Discover new information about alpacas.



# Index